Writing Lessons from the Front: Book 6

Plans and Processes

to get your book written

Angela Hunt

Hunt Haven
Press

Visit Angela Hunt's Web site at www.angelahuntbooks.com

ISBN: 0615852904
ISBN-13: 978-0615852904

"It takes as much energy to wish as it does to plan."
—Eleanor Roosevelt

1 THE ONE AND ONLY CHAPTER

I've always felt that being a writer is analogous to being a builder. A builder must know how to use the right tool at the right place in the right way, and he must know how to read and follow a blueprint. If he can do those things well, he can build anything from a doghouse to a Victorian mansion.

If a writer knows how to use the right tool at the right place in the right way, and if he knows how to read and follow the "blueprint" of every genre, he can write anything from a picture book to an epic novel.

I've been a professional writer for over thirty years, and I've written just about everything, including picture books and catalog copy and novels and collaborations and biographies and poetry and how-to books. I've always struggled to do my best, and I learned along the way.

You can, too.

This book will cover areas and concepts you should consider before, during, and after the writing. This lesson details the work a writer should do *away* from his or her manuscript—conceptualizing, identifying the genre, research, scheduling, drafting, critiquing, and publishing. So whether you want to write nonfiction or fiction, you should find something of value within these pages.

Nonfiction

Nonfiction is a broad umbrella that covers many different types of books, but the chief goal of nonfiction writers always seems to be *to impart information.* People who want to learn something head to the nonfiction section of their libraries and bookstores where they browse such diverse topics as how to feed their horses and how to find the best bargains at Disney World.

Yet nonfiction offers far more than how-to books. Biographies and autobiographies (memoirs) also fall into this category, as well as titles intended to persuade, entertain, and inform (including reference and textbooks). But no matter what your nonfiction topic, remember that *your book should have take-away value for the reader.* I've met many beginning writers at conferences who simply want to tell their story. They've been through something unusual or traumatic, and they're convinced that other people will find their story fascinating.

Well . . . maybe and maybe not. What people often fail to realize is that everyone has a story, and we are most keenly interested in our own stories. So if you want me to read and enjoy your story, I need to feel that I will somehow benefit from it.

Will I be entertained? Will I be inspired? Will I be challenged? Will I learn what you learned so I don't have to endure what you endured?

Will I learn the importance of trying to keep a marriage together? Or the wisdom of leaving an abusive husband? Will you offer me helpful tips and resources so I can accomplish what you accomplished?

If you're writing a biography, is the subject truly noteworthy? Does he or she provide an inspiring example for others? Could he or she be a role model?

If you're writing a book on the history of aviation, have you mingled enough true stories among the facts and diagrams that a layman would keep reading? People love to read about other people, so have you included interviews and anecdotes about brave pilots?

If you want to tell your life story, remember to think of your reader first and last. Even if you think the book will probably be of interest only to your grandchildren, ask yourself what they can learn from your life and then speak to them in such a way that they'll put down their iPads and cell phones to read your book.

No matter what your topic, take a minute to complete this little exercise:

My reader will receive _____ from my book.

I hope that blank was easy to fill in. Because if you're struggling to find a reason people would want to read your book, a publisher will struggle to find a reason to buy it.

I cut my teeth writing nonfiction. My novels, in fact, are almost always based in fact (which probably explains why I've never written a fantasy).

One of my first published books was on the topic of adoption. My husband and I worked so hard to adopt our children, I thought other couples would benefit from hearing our story.

But I quickly realized that every adoptive couple has a story, and many were just as interesting as ours. So my book had to offer something extra. I couldn't simply write up our story and call it quits.

I had to offer other interested couples a few practical tools. So in the back of the book I included a list of private adoption agencies from all fifty states. I also included a bibliography for further reading, and if the Internet had been around in those days, I would have included a list of helpful websites.

The take-away value of your book will depend, of course, on your topic and the type of nonfiction you are writing. But generally, personal stories do not sell unless

—you are a celebrity
—you have a large TV or radio platform
—or you offer tremendous take-away value for the reader.

"But I'm not worried about selling my book to a publisher," you may say. "I'm going to self-publish it."

Doesn't matter; the same rules apply. Unless you want your book to sit on Amazon with a scattering of five star reviews from your relatives and one-star reviews from everyone else, make sure you remember this: people will read, enjoy, and recommend your book only if they have received value from it.

Take a moment to let that sink in.

Maybe another moment.

Got it?

Okay. Now that you have considered and defined the value readers will gain from your book, visit the following website and locate your topic within the library Dewey Decimal system:

http://www.library.illinois.edu/ugl/about/dewey.html

If you wanted to write a book on the history and development

7

of pretzels, you would find your book placed at 641, under "Food and Drink."

If you have trouble deciding where your book would go, is it because you simply don't know where the library would put it, or is it because you haven't identified a clear topic? You could answer the first question by calling your local library and posing the question to a reference librarian. To answer the second question, you probably need to clarify the concept of your book and determine who would benefit most from it.

Because I heard this often at writers' conferences, I know some of you want to write the true story of your parents or grandparents but "in novel form." If that's your situation, ask yourself a couple of basic questions. First—are you willing to change the order of story events to tell a better story? (Fiction has to make sense; real life doesn't.) Second, are you going to change any names or fictionalize any part of the story?

If you are going to bend the truth a bit, you should either say so in an author's note at the end (*The author has taken liberties with certain dates, places, and identities in order to protect the innocent . . .*) or you could write the book as a novel.

If you write the book as a novel, however, you shouldn't insist on recording events "just as they happened." Ever wonder why most novels and movies have a notice that they were "*based upon actual events*" instead of claiming to be true stories? Because actual events rarely fit the blueprint for writing a novel, so history may need to be tweaked.

The Oscar-winning film "Chariots of Fire," for example, was based upon the true biography of Eric Liddell, an Olympic runner who later became a missionary to China. In the movie, Liddell's sister Jennie was portrayed as a bit of a nag—she didn't want him to focus on his running and was always chiding him about the Olympics. But in real life, Jennie Liddell was tremendously supportive of her brother. Why did the filmmakers cast her in such a negative light?

Because fiction thrives on conflict and without it, the story falls flat. Poor Jennie's reputation was sacrificed to story.

On the other hand, if you want to stick to the facts and record events as they actually happened, you can certainly do it in the *style* of a novel, you simply write what's called "creative nonfiction." Let me illustrate:

Factual reporting:
Melvin and Belinda Brown, my grandparents, arrived at Ellis Island in 1852. Melvin had been sick with the whooping cough while aboard ship, and Belinda had grown thin with running all over the ship seeking medicine for him. They settled in Philadelphia after Belinda saw the city's name on a poster and told Melvin she liked it.

Creative nonfiction style:
On a summer day in 1852, Melvin Stoddard stood at the railing of the S. S. Minnow and watched the Statue of Liberty appear on the horizon. "Look there," he told his wife Belinda, nudging her with his elbow. He glanced at her wan face and frowned. She had worn herself to a nub caring for him when he was sick, and for a while he worried that she'd catch the whooping cough herself. But his wife was stronger than she looked, and he could only be thankful that they'd both survived the crossing.

Later, as they walked down the ramp that led to Ellis Island, Belinda squeezed his arm and pointed to a poster featuring tall buildings and wide streets. "Phil-a-del-phi-a," she said, sounding out the word. "What a pretty name. If they let us choose, let's settle there."

How could he refuse? He owed her his life.

He covered her hand with his. "Whatever you want, dearest."

Writing in creative nonfiction, of course, means that you have to take a few liberties. You may know that your grandparents Melvin and Belinda arrived on a ship in 1852, but you don't know what Melvin actually said to her or if they watched the Statue of Liberty as they pulled into port. What you do in those cases is write what you believe is *plausible or likely*—and it's probably a good idea at the end of the book to include an author's note saying that you've "filled in the gaps" where necessary. But if you're writing creative nonfiction, you shouldn't change any major events you know to be true. When you do that on a large scale, you're writing fiction.

Always remember that *story* is valuable even in nonfiction. I was taken to church regularly as a child, and in those days most churches didn't offer programs geared to children. So I had to sit in the worship service with all the adults, and I'm pretty sure I had my head in my mother's lap for many a sermon. I slept, or tried to sleep, while she played with my hair or read her Bible along with the pastor.

But even as a preschooler, I remember sitting straight up, eyes wide, the minute the preacher launched into a story. He'd say, "The other night my wife . . ." and I perked up. Everyone else did, too. Or he'd tell a story about his childhood, or about one of his friends.

I can't remember much about those early sermons, but I do remember loving the preacher's stories. Humans are hard-wired to appreciate story, so it's a good idea to pepper your nonfiction book with anecdotes. Even something as simple as a recipe book—a collection of baking formulas and directions—can benefit from stories to introduce each recipe.

My husband loves "American Pickers" on the History Channel. I couldn't see what he found so fascinating about Mike and Frank picking through old junk until I watched a couple of episodes. It's not the junk that attracts people, but the *stories* people tell. After hearing those stories, those piles of junk become heaps of treasure.

So even in nonfiction, don't ignore the power of story. You'd be leaving a valuable writer's tool on the shelf.

Writing a Life Story
If you're writing the story of someone's life—your or someone else's—you may find the plot skeleton lesson useful. All good stories have the same bone structure, so you may discover that the life story you want to tell naturally fits the skeleton.

I've never written my life story (boring!), but I've written about episodes in my life and that's what I'd recommend to you, too. No one wants to read about every event in anyone's lifespan because we all go through long periods where nothing noteworthy happens. But everyone has stories about a specific event or time when something unusual happened—and that's a story worth writing.

On several occasions I've been hired to write a celebrity's story as a collaborative work. I've written with Deanna Favre, wife to football player Brett Favre; Mandisa; Heather Whitestone, Miss America 1995; Gayle Haggard; and a couple whose frozen embryo was transferred to another woman. In each situation, my client experienced an event that proved to be the "inciting incident" for a story. They formed goals, they faced complications, they endured bleakest moments and received help. And they learned lessons and made decisions that changed their lives forever, and those are the values and lessons the reader takes away from their stories.

All of the above terms will be familiar to you if you've read *The Plot Skeleton,* and if you haven't that little book will help you structure your story, too. Focus your story on one event, identify the plot elements that will make this story compelling and memorable, and identify the life lessons learned through this event. And there you have all the elements needed for a compelling life story.

Fiction

Fiction, of course, is all about story. A novel is a fictional exploration of a universal truth—as viewed by the author—consisting of narrative prose, a plot, a setting, and a theme. A novel is usually one character's story—it may offer a large cast and several point of view characters, but still, one character is dominant. A novel is a microcosm that says, "this is how the world is."

I wish I could come up with a more succinct definition, but I've tried. Since "universal truth" is a relative term these days, the author's worldview definitely comes into play. And though novels are fiction, meaning the events are not actual, novels focus on true characters, lessons, and moral values. A novel that does not present both sides to a moral argument descends to the level of propaganda.

My novel *The Pearl* deals with cloning after a woman's five-year-old son is killed in a freak accident. Because she is a radio personality, a group known for promoting cloning offers to clone her son. She is so desperate to regain her beloved child that she considers the offer.

When I began writing *The Pearl,* I knew that as a Christian I ought to be opposed to cloning, but why? I wasn't sure. After all, if we can clone a liver and transplant it into a dying man, why not support cloning?

So I had my protagonist do some serious investigation in the matter, and I was careful to uncover as many pro-cloning as anti-cloning arguments.

At the end of the story, it's not facts and figures that make her decide to turn down the cloning offer. She says no because she sees firsthand what the technology leads to when combined with selfish human desires. If I had completely avoided the pro-cloning side of the argument, I don't think it would have been an honest book.

The purpose of a novel is not to impart facts (although learning new things is often a pleasant side effect of reading fiction), but to evoke emotion.

Let's break this down. Novels usually have one protagonist. A novel with two protagonists (*A Thousand Splendid Suns, A Tale of Two Cities, The Face*), will often feature a main character who sacrifices himself for the other, so only one character remains at the ending. Why only one?

I once decided to try my hand at an "ensemble novel." In *Uncharted*, I would feature six main characters, and I would weight them equally. No character would be more important than the others.

Which meant I was dealing with six different plotlines, or plot skeletons. Which meant I had six different inciting incidents, six different goals, six different characters facing complications . . . you get the idea.

When I had finished the rough draft, I had a long book that felt repetitive. I carried it with me to a writer's workshop led by Donald Maass, who wisely pointed out that even in an ensemble cast, one character needs to be predominant. So I chose one out of the six, recast the story from her perspective, and that move turned a convoluted story into an especially haunting one.

By having six main characters, I was also diluting my reader's bond with the protagonist. Readers want to identify with the main character, and if a writer has more than one strong main character, readers literally divide their loyalties. This dilutes the reading experience. The closer you want to bind your reader to your protagonist, the shorter your list of point of view characters should be.

Likewise, the broader the topic, the smaller your point of view needs to be. Someone once said, "If you want to write about war, write about one man's war."

I remember sitting my friend Lori Copeland's living room on September 11, 2001. I had been about to go to the airport to fly home, but after the planes crashed into the Twin Towers, I realized I wouldn't be going anywhere.

As we sat in silence watching the formerly awesome towers crumble into dust, I remember thinking that the situation was overwhelming, simply too awful. How could anyone ever write about it? The tragedy, the devastation, the horror of all those people struggling for their lives in three separate locations . . .

Yet people have written successfully about 9/11 . . . through the eyes of *one* person. When a tragedy or situation is so huge you struggle to grasp all its implications, go into the head of one person affected by the event and write the story from his or her perspective.

I once had only a few minutes to talk to a woman about her manuscript in progress. Hoping she'd be succinct, I asked the usual opening question: "What's your story about?"

"It's about a woman," she answered, "who is abducted."

"Ah." I nodded. "So the book's about how she tries to get away from her kidnappers?"

The woman shook her head. "She spends most of the book locked up in an old house. But there's this detective—"

"So the story is about the detective and how he tries to outwit the kidnapper?"

She shook her head again. "The woman's boyfriend is a lawyer, and he's tied in with the kidnappers . . ."

"So it's the boyfriend's story, and he's frustrated by the police and trying to find her—"

She shook her head a third time.

At that point, I understood her problem—she couldn't pinpoint her protagonist. If you can't identify whose story you're telling, you need to go back to the starting line and ask yourself *whose point of view will help me write the most dramatic and emotional story?* I've gone back and started again, and believe me, it's worth the retreat.

Look over your cast of story characters and choose one to be the protagonist. The other characters will still play a role, of course, but the story should focus on one person—his hopes, fears, struggles, and desires.

Evaluating Your Idea
The late Gary Provost used to say that great ideas are like WAGS—and I've never forgotten his acronym. As you consider whether your story idea is strong enough for a full novel, consider these four elements:

W: World. Would this story transport the reader to another world? I don't mean Pluto or Mars, but any world the reader would find interesting. The world of high finance. The world of the Amazon rain forest. The world of a gorilla's zookeeper. The world of a woman with breast cancer. The world of ancient Persia.

People read to escape their ordinary lives, so don't let your protagonist spend most of his time in the ordinary world.

Lars and the Real Girl is one of my favorite movies. The film is set in a small town somewhere in Minnesota, and it's an ordinary small town until Lars, a painfully shy young man, orders a life-size anatomically correct adult doll . . . and believes she's real. The entire town enters into a kindly conspiracy to support Lars's delusion until, as his psychiatrist says, "he doesn't need it any more." The little town may look ordinary, but it's not because it's a community where Bianca the doll goes to church, reads to sick children at the hospital, and occupies a seat on the school board.

So wherever your story takes us, make sure it's a world your reader is likely to find different and interesting.

A: Active characters. Make certain your protagonist is not a navel-gazer. He or she must be willing to get up and do something to reach his goal.

I nearly wrote myself into a corner when I began to write *The Awakening*, a novel about a woman who suffers from agoraphobia. Aurora lived in the top floor of a Manhattan apartment building, and she hadn't stepped foot outside the building in over ten years. And there I was, writing a story about a woman too frightened to go anywhere or do anything.

So I had to make an adjustment. And that leads us to the next letter:

G: Goals. Active characters set goals, and if you are familiar with the plot skeleton, you'll recognize this event as one that occurs just after the inciting incident. As I was writing *The Awakening*, I sent Aurora to the rooftop, where she heard an audible voice from out of nowhere—her inciting incident. After hearing that voice—and believing that perhaps someone cared—she set the goal of trying to go down five additional steps of the staircase each day. An insignificant goal for most people, but Aurora wasn't most people. I showed her struggling, perspiring, and trembling as every day she worked up enough courage to descend five steps farther than she had the day before.

S: Stakes. Your protagonist must have a lot at stake during his venture. Ask yourself, "What would happen if my protagonist didn't meet his goal?" If your answer is, "Life would just go back to the way it was," your stakes aren't high enough. Your main character needs to burn some bridges so he can't go back unless he's victorious.

Remember me mentioning that I sent Aurora up to the rooftop in *The Awakening*? The story opens with her mother's funeral— Aurora has been her mother's nurse for the past ten years. And now that she is free to develop and enjoy a life of her own, she is imprisoned by her fears. So she goes up to the rooftop, fully intending to jump off, and is actually sitting on the ledge when she hears the voice from out of nowhere . . .

What is at stake? My reader knows that if Aurora doesn't meet her goals and conquer her agoraphobia, she's going to go back to the roof and finish what she started. Her life is riding on this venture.

What's at stake in nearly every James Bond film? The fate of the free world, of course. What's at stake in every story involving a kidnap victim? The victim's life. Sometimes a marriage or a detective's life are at risk, too. The more you put at stake, the better your story will be.

Using those four elements—WAGS—you can create a storyline in minutes. I'll pull some things from the top of my head, but you give it a try, too.

W: different world: um . . . the world of fashion shoe design.

A: active character: an ambitious young woman, fresh from fashion design school, wins the opportunity to intern at a famous Italian shoe design company.

G: goal: when she discovers that someone has been leaking copies of the famous designer's shoes to an American competitor, she determines to find the culprit.

S: stakes: as she snoops to discover the villain, she is discovered—and, depending upon the genre and age of the intended reader, either her reputation, her career, her life, or all three will be threatened.

See how it works? Now apply those four guidelines to your story and see how it measures up. Most stories fall short in the area of "high stakes"—we tend to shelter our protagonists and don't torture them nearly enough. Make sure your protagonist goes through the fire so at the end of the story he will either be worthy of his victory or sadder and much, much wiser.

Genres

Before you begin writing your novel, you should know which genre you're writing in. The number one mistake of beginning writers in this area is to not consider genre at all. Publishers have seasonal "lists" or catalogs to fill, and they may have room for two romances, three suspense novels, a western, and maybe one literary novel. Many genre readers are fanatically loyal—they'll read six or seven romances a month, or every mystery novel in a particular series. You should want your book to fill one of those available genre slots.

If you're writing a general novel, know that it can be harder to place a book in this category. An editor may love it, but if the sales and marketing folks don't know where the bookstores are going to put it, they're not going to be encouraging. And yes, the sales and marketing people do have a voice is whether or not your book is contracted.

I'm going to attempt to list some of the commonly accepted genres here, though they do change and shift over time. See if you can determine which category would best suit your novel:

Romance: a story in which the romantic plot is the primary plot. The man and woman *always* get together at the end. If they don't, it's not a genre romance.
    Historical Romance
    Military Romance

Cowboy Romance
Inspirational Romance (includes a strong faith element, almost always Christian)
Romantic Suspense
Supernatural Romance

Fantasy (can include time-travel)
Historical
Military/Spy novels
Westerns
Contemporary
Literary
Horror
Women's Fiction: features adult women, often married, dealing with contemporary issues
Chick Lit: feature twenty-something heroines in search of love
Science Fiction/Futuristic (includes Dystopian)
Bonnet books: feature small Amish or Mennonite communities
Faith Fiction or Christian fiction: Christian faith is an intrinsic part of the plot

Each genre has its own conventions, and you shouldn't knowingly violate them if you want to sell your manuscript. You wouldn't send a romantic story where the man and woman part ways to a romance editor, for instance, and you wouldn't send a story about a Buddhist to a publisher of Christian fiction. If you want to write within a specific genre, read several books in that genre so you can learn what the conventions are.

Some genres fade away over time. I included Chick Lit on the list because it was so popular a few years ago (pink and green covers, first person, present tense, young girl who loves shopping and the big city), but as of this writing the genre's popularity is fading. Bonnet books are huge right now, but I predict the genre will morph into "small town" books, because I believe what readers are seeking is escape into a small, friendly, non-threatening environment like Mayberry, R.F.D.

So do your research. Visit libraries and book stores to find out what is currently selling. What genres appear on your bookstore shelves? (If they shelve by genre—some smaller stores shelve by author's last name.) Make sure you have a clear idea of what genre your book will sell in, because that's the bottom line. Where will your book fit on that bookstore shelf?

Finding Time to Write

How do you eat a cow? One bite at a time.

Many people are overwhelmed by the mere idea of writing a book. But it's not difficult when you think of it as writing a page a day. If you began today, a year from now you'd have 365 pages, a fairly hefty novel. If even that seems overwhelming, ask yourself what you'll have a year from now if you *don't* do anything to begin your book.

A page a day is a simplistic idea, however, because you will need several days of research and preparation. You'll also have days where you're in the groove and you'll write five pages, or even ten. Or maybe you'll get one of those delicious three-day weekends and somehow get an entire day to yourself—you may write three chapters!

I'm like most of you—busy. I have a family with children and a grandchild, I have two puppies who can be demanding, I try to exercise consistently, I clean my own home, I attend my church, I lead a neighborhood book club, I travel frequently, and I volunteer at my community animal shelter every week. I know you have a busy schedule, too.

But over the years, I've learned an important principle: we find time to do the things we really want to do. And if you really want to write a book, you can find the time.

Here's how.

Go to your computer and open your calendar program. Print out copies of the next few months. With the printed pages before you, put a slash through all the days you know you absolutely cannot work on your book. (I routinely mark through travel days, Saturdays, and some holidays. And my birthday.)

Now look at the remaining days and ask yourself where you can find a block of two or three free hours. Week nights? Sunday afternoons? Saturday mornings?

I have one friend who got up an hour early every morning to write her first book. I'm not sure I could think at five a.m., but she knew she'd be able to get her book done while the rest of the household slept. Maybe that will be your productive time, too.

Look for your open blocks of time, and block them out.

Consider them sacrosanct, appointments you have with your book. Now, on that printed calendar, give yourself a goal for each block of time. It can be as simple as "research colonial period" or "write five pages" or "edit pages 4-13." If you're just starting out, though, you'll want to pencil in days for plotting, character development, and research.

More on what you'll be writing later. But first let's talk about the work of preparation.

Research

Whether you are writing fiction or nonfiction, you will have to do some research. You will have to read a lot of material on your nonfiction topic, and if you're writing a novel set in a real town, you'd better learn some street names and a bit of history about that town. If an issue arises in your book, you will have to be well-read on the latest information about that topic.

I've written several books that were fairly research-intensive, and people always ask how long it took me to do the research. They always look surprised when I tell them it only took a week or two.

Research can be like quicksand. You can get caught in it. The amount of material available, combined with the primal fear of the blank screen, can entice you to postpone the actual writing of your book far longer than necessary. Research can fritter away weeks, even months, until you forget the material you read when you began the research work.

So I advise this: spend a few days gathering as much information as you can. Print out *trustworthy* information from the Internet (that rules out a lot of material on Wikipedia), buy or borrow books, clip articles, look for YouTube videos on the topic. Then compile this information into a notebook, or make notes of where the information can be found.

(Note: when I saw "a few days" keep in mind that writing is a fulltime job for me, so I'm talking about forty hours or so of research. If you write when you can find a couple of hours here and there, you may need more than a few days.)

Next, read enough to get the Big Picture of whatever it is you're researching—social customs in medieval times, prion diseases, foreign adoption, in vitro fertilization, Cuban groceries, whatever. If you're setting your novel in a real location, use Google earth to get a bird's eye view of the town and zoom in on the house where you think your character would live. Print out a photo and keep it in your notebook. Take about a week to do this "macro" round of research.

Once you have a good understanding of the subjects involved in your book, spend some hours researching your characters. Figure out their personality type and create a personality profile for them (more on this in *Creating Extraordinary Characters.*) If your protagonist will be employed in an occupation you don't know well, do some research on what would be involved in your character's daily work. Is he a trial lawyer? A brain surgeon? Find a brain surgeon or lawyer who might be willing to sit for an interview or look at your manuscript to check for anything implausible. Sometimes it's far easier to give your characters an occupation you know well—that's why so many literary lawyers write legal thrillers.

Once you have a good handle on your subject and your protagonist's occupation, take some time to research the setting. If this is a real town, you can visit it (and claim expenses as tax deductions if you sell your book) or learn as much as you can through online research. If you're creating a fictional town, you will still need to establish a few details: where is it located? What state? Will your plot require you to know any particular laws of that state? What are the signs of seasonal change?

As you research, don't spend too much time gathering details. You can always go back and find the missing detail you need, but it will be impossible to gather every detail up front because you won't really know what you need until you finish the first draft.

When I'm first drafting, I will do almost anything to avoid stopping the flow of words onto my computer screen. If my characters sit down to eat in medieval England, I'll write something like:

> All eyes focused on King Henry as he took his place at the center of the table. Four servants brought in a steaming tray of [find out what the king would eat at a banquet], and the guests burst into applause.

I'll talk more about those brackets later, but you get the idea. Press on. You can always look up details later.

Drafting

When you think you've allowed enough time for your research tasks, pick up your calendar and look at the next blocks of available time. You're nearly ready to begin writing.

Before you do, however, you might want to pick up a package of note cards. Many writers—including me—find it useful to use note cards to represent scenes (fiction) or chapters (nonfiction) in the book we're about to write. Working either from a plot skeleton (fiction) or an outline (nonfiction), we use the notecards to very briefly sketch out either what will happen in a scene or what topics we plan to hit in this chapter. The beauty of using notecards is that you can tape them to the wall and move them around as other ideas come to you.

So if you like the idea of notecards, pencil in a day or two to write up your notecards for your book. If you're writing a novel, you may need sixty or more scenes, so don't feel that you have to do them all at once. But at least try to sketch out your scenes for the first part of the book: in plot skeleton parlance, that means you'll sketch out scenes from the beginning through the inciting incident and the establishment of the goal.

If you've purchased colored note cards, you might want to use pink cards for your heroine and blue for her love interest. But do whatever suits you.

When you've done your note cards, you are ready to begin writing. Take a deep breath and don't let the Fear of the Blank Screen postpone your efforts one more day.

Pick up your printed calendar, look at your next available writing blocks, and give yourself a word count goal for each. I don't know how fast you write; you're going to have to figure this one out yourself. But remember—a first draft is not a polished draft, so these don't have to be beautiful or fancy words. They're just words on the page, that's all. When I'm first-drafting, in an eight hour day I can slap between five and seven thousand words onto the screen.

But I wouldn't want anyone to read them.

The secret to getting a first draft finished is *not* to go back and edit—or if you absolutely cannot control the urge, then only look at the material you wrote the day before. Some folks spend all their time editing the book they *could finish* if they didn't spend all their time editing.

I've always felt that producing a first draft was like birthing a baby. First-drafting is my least favorite part of writing because it's doggone hard work—you are pulling story from of thin air. The process involves a lot of pain and suffering and panting and grumbling and occasional yelling, but when that baby is on the table, you're done. It may be a bloody mess, but it's alive and squalling, and you've done the hard work.

Now all you have to do is clean it up—and that's what subsequent drafts are about.

Whenever I teach, people always ask about my drafting/revision system, so I'm happy to explain it here. I write in layers because the more time I spend with a book, the better I know my characters and the deeper I can take my story. At the end of my first draft—which might be only half the length of a finished book—I finally feel that I know what my story is about and who my characters are. The plot skeleton doesn't give me that—it only provides a framework for what my story might become. The first draft wraps that skeleton in flesh, and it's the subsequent drafts that fatten the story up, clothe it in mystery or magic or humor, and deepen the theme.

Between every draft, I take a day or two for what I once heard Sol Stein call "triage." First, I go back through the manuscript and search for [, the left bracket, because those are the spots where I know I need to look something up. I take the time to find out what King Henry would eat at his medieval dinner, I look up the name of a cemetery in Kennebunkport, etc. Whatever details I now know I'll need, I take the time to look them up.

I also fill in any obvious gaps. Suppose I realized in chapter seventeen that Thomas has a twin brother. I can't suddenly introduce this brother in chapter seventeen; that's much too late. So I need to include the brother in an early scene, perhaps at the family reunion in chapter four. So I'll go back to chapter four and write in the brother, give him a name and a charming disposition, and add whatever else I need to add.

If you've done a plot skeleton, as I always do, you have plenty of room for discovery along the journey. Trust me, you will discover story developments that simply didn't occur to you when you first began plotting. So this triage time is useful for making notes in the margins (the "insert comment" command in Microsoft

Word is good for this) or whatever else you need to do.

When you are ready to begin your second draft, your story should be in fairly good shape. You have a plot with a beginning, middle, and (hopefully) an end. When you take out your calendar to schedule work on your second draft, you can no longer gauge your progress by word count, nor can you use the computer's page count—it will change as soon as you begin to add new material. So you should print out a copy of your first draft and be sure to number the pages. As you work on your second draft, assign yourself a certain number of pages to edit per work block. Again, the number of pages you assign depends completely on how much time you have available and how quickly you work.

At this point, I can't tell you how many drafts to do. Some writers do over twenty drafts of some sections, others do three. I usually do four or five, depending on how much I struggled with making the story conform to what I imagined it to be. But with each subsequent draft my focus shifts from being story-centered to being detail-centered. My first drafts are all about shaping story; my later drafts are more about cleaning up the language and listening to the rhythm of the words.

So I'll tell you what I do, but you work according to the way you're wired.

As I mentioned, my second draft is all about filling in gaps, doing the detailed research, and making sure the story and characters are complete. By the time it's finished, the manuscript may be about three-quarters of its final length.

During my third draft, I focus on creating "mood music." If a scene is suspenseful, I might change it from daytime to evening; I might clear everyone out of the house, I might have thunder rumbling in the distance—or write in a power outage. Whatever suits the scene. If a scene is "loud," I might rewrite it so that it's quiet and more intense. I want to be sure each scene is set in the best location, at the best time, and is suited for eliciting emotion from my reader.

From the third draft forward, I use the search/replace feature of my word processing program to search out and edit weasel words.

I have my computer read the manuscript to me during the fourth draft. Apple computers have speech built in; PC users can always download Adobe Reader and use it to have the computer read a selection to them. Your ear will pick up repeated words, flat dialogue, and missing words much better than your eye will. You could read the pages aloud, but your eye will probably skip over all the mistakes it didn't see when the pages were on your computer.

While the computer reads a scene to me, I hold the printed pages in my hand and mark it quickly so I don't fall behind. I circle words that don't work, I write "rep" next to repeated words that strike my ear, and I write FIX in the margin if a passage simply isn't working. After I've listened to each scene, I go back and make those changes on the computer.

I usually set the manuscript aside for a couple of days before beginning the final draft, and during those days I ask myself if I've developed the theme enough . . . if my protagonist is sympathetic enough . . . and if the reader will take away what I want them to take away. Then I read through the manuscript fairly quickly just to make sure I've done all I can do.

Honestly, by this point I am dizzy with the story and the process. I am so close to it that I can't tell if it's the best thing I've ever written or the worst. All I can do is make sure it's the best and cleanest I can make it, and then I send it off to my agent.

As you write, you will develop your own processes. Some of my methods may work for you, some may seem like a lot of fuss and bother. We're all different, and thank goodness we are.

But if you have struggled to produce a complete manuscript, if you have found it difficult to set aside time for writing, I hope some of these suggestions will help you.

Time Management

If you habitually struggle with finding time for anything, I have a few tips that might prove helpful—they've certainly helped me.

1. Realize that you don't have to answer the phone. If the call is important, the caller can leave a message. You pay for telephone service, so you are the boss.
2. Learn to say no. Scarlett O'Hara had a little speech memorized for occasions when men proposed to her. It went something like, "Kind sir, I am not unaware of the honor you have bestowed upon me by asking me to be your wife, but I cannot in good conscience accept your offer . . ."

You should come up with a similar speech when you're

asked to head a charity drive or take an extra week for carpool or bake four dozen cookies for the bake sale. If the request interferes with your writing time, you should say, "Dear friend, I am not unaware of the honor you have bestowed upon me by asking me to participate in your endeavor . . ." Well, you get the idea.

3. Tame the television. Trust me, even with 500 channels, television isn't so compelling that you must watch it every night. Pick out the shows you really enjoy and watch those, but turn the thing off for everything else.

4. Capture stolen moments. When you find yourself waiting at the doctor's office, sitting in the carpool line, or standing in the queue at Starbucks, pull out the book you're reading for research or pop in your ear buds to listen to an audio book. Either option is a good way to redeem your lost time.

5. Have a particular place to write. You'll save time if you don't have to "set up" your desk, computer, dictionary, music, whatever you use to get in the flow.

6. Remember this principle: your life consists of a finite succession of moments. Wasting time is literally wasting your life.

7. Harness the power of the carrot. Yep, you're the toiling donkey, so what will you use to reward yourself at the end of your writing time? A cold Diet Coke? A nap? Playtime with the puppy?

8. Remember that multi-tasking is a myth. When most people say they are multi-tasking, they are actually switch-tasking, shifting from one task to another. This is not an effective way to do anything.

In the 1740s, Lord Chesterfield offered the following advice to his son: "There is time enough for everything in the course of the day if you do but one thing at once, but there is not time enough in the year if you will do two things at a time."[1] So when you're writing, focus on the writing.

Critique, Anyone?

Though I have never been part of a writers' group, many people swear that they are wonderful, supportive, and helpful. Some participate in local groups; others find critique groups online. If you think the experience would be something you'd enjoy, call your local library to ask if they know of writers' groups in your community.

If you join a group, however, make sure the group is building you up, not tearing you down. I've heard horror stories about jealousy and destructive criticism that fatally injured fledgling writers just as they were about to fly.

Years ago I read an anecdote in *Reader's Digest* that I've never forgotten. Seems a young husband watched his wife cook a ham, but was mystified when she cut off both ends before placing it in the oven. When he asked why she did it, she said, "Because my mother always did."

So they called Mom, asked her the same question, and got the same answer: "Because *my* mother always did."

So the newlyweds called Grandma and asked why she cut off both ends of the ham before baking. "Simple," she said. "My baking dish was too small for the ham."

That story reminds me of tales I've heard about critique group experiences. Someone in the group—someone who may be unpublished or self-published—will say that something *must* be written in such-and-such an way, and everyone will believe that pronouncement whether or not it is true.

Critique groups have their own jargon. I've been around other writers who talk about RUE (resist the urge to explain) and SDT (show, don't tell) as casually as chefs talk about spices. I had to laugh at one conference when a teaching friend told me that someone in her class had asked when "STDs were appropriate." Maybe *never?*

I've met with far too many writers who have been henpecked by critique groups who obey rules that are like Grandma's undersized baking pan. Sometimes these groups can be adamant about what can and cannot be done, and often they are the blind leading the blind.

I've discovered a condition I call Critique Group Dependency. I've read manuscripts that could have sparkled with verve, but the writer's critique groups scrubbed all the sparkle away. I've talked to writers at conferences who hesitantly told me, "My critique group feels this is too ____ (insert adjective), but I think it's what I want to say." I've seen manuscripts where the author second-guessed every other line based on feedback from her critique group.

Let me assure you—a writer's voice must be confident. At some point you have to trust yourself and block out other critics. Writing is a craft and an art, and sometimes the art overrules the craft. Yes, there are rules, but sometimes they can and should be broken. If you have to break them, break them boldly and be able to explain the reason for your choices.

If your critique group offers a suggestion and you are persuaded by their logic, fine, they've been helpful. But if they offer a suggestion that goes against all your instincts, thank them and forget it. Those folks around the table are not editors, they're writers, and *no one* is more critical about writing than another writer.

Trust me, nothing substitutes for experience. Listen to those who have been published many times; read books by editors and writers who know the ropes. Take all other advice lightly.

Another subtle danger lurks in critique groups—the danger of over-exposing the book that's dear to your heart. You can talk the magic and enthusiasm right out of your work if you're not careful. Or others could pick it to death and leave your darling looking like a Persian cat left out in the rain.

So be careful. If you think you might like to join a critique group, attend the first meeting and listen. See if the comments made about submitted work is constructive or destructive. What is the experience level of the other writers? Are they committed to helping each other, or are they primarily looking out for themselves?

I know wonderful critique groups exist. If you find a good one, count yourself fortunate and enjoy the feedback that should help you write a better book. I frequently use test readers, and their feedback is always valuable.

But I also know how criticism can sting. Most of us can read twenty wonderful comments and one negative, and it's the negative one that keeps us awake at night. So develop a thick skin, brace yourself, and make sure your manuscript is as polished as possible before you send it out into the world.

Writing is an act of bravery, after all.

Traditional or Self-Publishing

I didn't feel this book would be complete without discussing traditional and self-publishing. Writers today have more choices

27

than ever, but you need to be fully informed in order to make the best choice possible.

Traditional publishing has a lot to recommend it. Writers become traditionally published when they submit a manuscript either directly to the publisher or to an agent who submits it to the traditional publishing house (many large houses won't accept unagented manuscripts). Manuscripts accepted by traditional publishing are usually the crème de la crème—acquisitions editors look for books that are well written and should sell to a large number of people. After acquiring the book, an editor at the publishing house will go through the manuscript and advise the writer about how to do a rewrite—yes, another draft. When that is complete, usually the same editor will do a line edit: he or she will go through the manuscript line by line, checking every word. After that, a copy editor will go through the work checking every fact, every spelling, and every punctuation mark. (Surprising, isn't it, that some typos still get through?) No wonder traditional publishing is still the ultimate dream for most writers.

Perhaps the most important consideration to a writer is that a traditional publishing house typically *pays the author an advance*, depending upon the projected sales of the book in the first year. The author pays nothing. The advance is supposed to give the writer money to live on while he's polishing the book and working on his next one.

After the book is completely edited, it will be professionally designed and typeset, then sent to the printer. During this process, a sales and marketing team will discuss the book and make plans for how they can best sell it. Years ago, virtually all marketing and publicity was handled by the publishing house (not surprising, since they don't want to lose the money they've invested in the project.) Today, however, most publishers expect the author to bear a large part of the marketing burden. Authors are expected to maintain audiences on Facebook, Twitter, and Pinterest. They are also expected to send regular newsletters to keep readers interested in their books.

The traditional publishers definitely have the upper hand when it comes to distribution. They have staff who handle the major sales channels—bookstore chains, large bookstores, Wal-Mart, Costco, Amazon, etc. These connections are already in place, so bookstores are told that new releases are coming, and many sales outlets place pre-orders in anticipation of a book's release date. Naturally, large pre-orders means lots of interest, and that's is welcome news for the publisher and the author.

When the book is finally released—usually anywhere from eight months to a year after it is submitted—it is distributed to major bookstores and online retailers and placed on sale. The author hopes his earned royalties exceed the amount of the advance he was given—if it does, he will earn more royalties for as long as the book remains for sale. If it does not, the publisher will take the loss, and they will probably not be as eager to spend as much for the author's *second* book.

The advent of the ebook has drastically changed the publishing world. Even large publishers now are finding it difficult to stay afloat, and they are becoming far pickier about the books they choose to publish. Furthermore, the number of publishers is shrinking as more publishing houses merge.

Years ago, any writer who wanted to publish his own book had to spend thousands of dollars and find a place to store thousands of books (the more you ordered, the lower the price per book). "Vanity presses" abounded, and editors at these presses were not picky. They would print about anything that came to them, and very little real editing was done. The writer paid for everything, and though the subsidy publisher promised to market and distribute the book, very often this amounted to a mention in the company catalog and/or a listing at Amazon.com (do you realize how many books are listed on Amazon.com?).

Technology has dramatically changed self-publishing. The rise of the POD press (print on demand) has made it possible for writers to upload a book online, place it for sale on Amazon.com and other websites, and collect a steady trickle of royalties without any major upfront costs. Different POD programs offer different options, and many of them charge plenty for their editorial services, but theoretically a writer could self-publish cheaply.

The only problem is that most of these books are awful. They are written by people who have never studied the craft, they are not well edited, and the covers often look homemade. The books make it onto Amazon, true, and a few of the writer's friends and family may leave glowing reviews, but those review don't improve the quality of the book.

I'm not writing this to condemn self-publishing—the book

you're reading now was self-published. But if you are interested in self-publishing, *please* do all you can to produce a quality product. If you want to sell more than one title, and especially if you hope to have any kind of career as a writer, learn how to write well, hire an editor, have a professional design your cover, and run your material by some test readers before you submit it.

Also be aware that you alone will be responsible for promoting, marketing, and distributing your book. You may not have to warehouse books in your garage, but you'll have to partner with a POD printer who is willing to print and ship books for you. It's a lot of work, and just because a book is on Amazon.com doesn't mean it will sell itself.

I have nothing against self-publishing. A lawyer friend of mine wrote a book on Florida law and self-published it successfully because he knew no traditional publisher would want to publish a book that would only be of interest to residents of the Sunshine State. I self-published this series of writing lessons because I wanted to try the *a la carte* approach and knew no traditional publisher would be interested in publishing a series of booklets. I've also self-published some of my traditionally-published books that have gone out of print—a situation that probably won't occur any more because digital and print on demand books can stay "in print" forever.

Yet too many people are publishing books without spending a single hour studying the craft of writing. They're writing books without studying the "blueprints" of their genre. People call themselves *author* without investing an ounce of blood, sweat, or tears—just a few dollars.

They don't know what they're missing.

I'll wrap up this little section with a story: in his book *The Genius In All of Us: New Insights Into Genetics, Talent, and IQ*, David Shenk cites Stanford psychologist Walter Mischel's study of a particular group of four year olds. In the 1970s, he gathered them together and offered the children a choice: they could have one marshmallow immediately or wait a little while (while Mischel "ran an errand") for two marshmallows. The results:

*one-third of the kids immediately took the single marshmallow.

*one-third waited a few minutes but then gave in and settled for the single marshmallow.

*one-third patiently waited fifteen minutes for two marshmallows.

After fourteen years, Mischel checked in with the same subjects again. He compared the SAT scores of the original nonwaiting group to the waiting group and found the latter scored an average of 210 points higher.

> Those with an early capacity for self-discipline and delayed gratification had gone on to much higher academic success. The delayed-gratification kids were also rated as much better able to cope with social and personal problems.[2]

Why am I telling stories about children and marshmallows? Because the chief problem with self-published books is that they were published *too soon*. The writer hasn't taken the time to hone his skills, nor had he tested his material with a critique group, an early reader, or an acquisitions editor. When you hear an editor say, "I would love to publish this, but simply don't have a place for it in my list," then you know you're ready to publish in any venue.

The notion of *deliberate practice*, also explored by Shenk, says that aspiring performers concentrate on improving their work by engaging in practice activities designed to change and refine particular mechanisms. In other words, clarifies Shenk, "it is practice that doesn't take no for an answer; practice that perseveres; the type of practice where the individual keeps raising the bar of what he or she considers success."[3]

How can you engage in deliberate practice? You find a writers group and endure solid critique without flinching. You read books on the craft of writing—and by reading this book, you're already doing that. You attend writing workshops and conferences. You enter your work into legitimate contests. (My first book was published because it won a contest.) You submit your work to magazines, online sites, and book publishers. You listen to feedback and work specifically on the areas where you have weaknesses.

Don't think that everything you do has to be centered on the one book you're working on. When I started, for the first five years I wrote anything anyone asked me to write—radio copy, catalog copy, articles, reports, interviews, personality profiles—and then I saw an ad about a children's picture book contest. Before I even thought about what sort of book I would write, I went to the library and borrowed a book on how to write children's picture books—and believe me, there's a blueprint. I learned that picture books are usually thirty-two pages and under 1,000 words, so that's what I wrote. And that story became my first published book.

When you're told that your novel has too much backstory, or that your nonfiction book is confusing, don't get defensive, just thank the person who was brave enough to offer their comments and look at your work with a critical eye. Were the comments justified? If so, how can you cut the backstory or clarify your material?

How can you make your work shine so that it stands out amid other manuscripts in the slush pile or sparkles amid the flood of self-published books on Amazon?

Publishers and editors want you to succeed because they need good books to publish. *I* want you to succeed because I need good books to read. But success often means that you're going to have to wait and work a while before you can have those two marshmallows.

So what are you waiting for? Start writing!

Thank you for purchasing this book in **Writing Lessons from the Front.** If you find any typos in this book, please write and let us know where they are: hunthaven@gmail.com.

We would also appreciate it if you would be kind enough to leave a review of this book on Amazon. Thank you!

ABOUT THE AUTHOR

Angela Hunt writes for readers who have learned to expect the unexpected from this versatile writer. With over four million copies of her books sold worldwide, she is the best-selling author of more than 120 works ranging from picture books (*The Tale of Three Trees*) to novels and nonfiction.

Now that her two children have reached their twenties, Angie and her husband live in Florida with Very Big Dogs (a direct result of watching *Turner and Hooch* too many times). This affinity for mastiffs has not been without its rewards—one of their dogs was featured on *Live with Regis and Kelly* as the second-largest canine in America. Their dog received this dubious honor after an all-expenses-paid trip to Manhattan for the dog and the Hunts, complete with VIP air travel and a stretch limo in which they toured New York City. Afterward, the dog gave out pawtographs at the airport.

Angela admits to being fascinated by animals, medicine, unexplained phenomena, and "just about everything." Books, she says, have always shaped her life— in the fifth grade she learned how to flirt from reading *Gone with the Wind*.

Her books have won the coveted Christy Award, several Angel Awards from Excellence in Media, and the Gold and Silver Medallions from *Foreword Magazine*'s Book of the Year Award. In 2007, her novel *The Note* was featured as a Christmas movie on the Hallmark channel. She recently completed her doctorate in biblical literature and is now finishing her doctorate in Theology.

When she's not home writing, Angie often travels to teach writing workshops at schools and writers' conferences. And to talk about her dogs, of course. Readers may visit her web site at www.angelahuntbooks.com.

Selected Novels by Angela Hunt

The Offering
The Fine Art of Insincerity
Five Miles South of Peculiar
The Face
Let Darkness Come
The Elevator
The Novelist
The Awakening
The Truth Teller
Unspoken
Uncharted
The Justice
The Canopy
The Immortal
Doesn't She Look Natural?
She Always Wore Red
She's In a Better Place
The Pearl
The Note
The Debt
Then Comes Marriage
The Shadow Women
Dreamers
Brothers
Journey
Roanoke
Jamestown
Hartford
Rehoboth
Charles Towne
The Proposal
The Silver Sword
The Golden Cross
The Velvet Shadow
The Emerald Isle

ENDNOTES

[1] Lord Chesterfield quoted in Christine Rosen's "The Myth of Multitasking," *The New Atlantis*, http://www.thenewatlantis.com/publications/the-myth-of-multitasking .

[2] Davie Shenk, *The Genius in All of Us: Why Everything You've Been told About Genetics, Talent, and IQ is Wrong* (New York: Doubleday, 2011).

[3] Shenk, op.cit.

3738180R00021

Made in the USA
San Bernardino, CA
17 August 2013